A Belbin Book

First published in 2008 by Belbin

Copyright © BELBIN, 2008, 2009, 2012, 2013

The moral right of the authors has been asserted.

ISBN 978-0-9552979-5-3

Printed and bound by Moreton Hall Press, Suffolk
www.moretonhallpress.co.uk

Belbin
3-4 Bennell Court
West Street
Comberton
Cambridge
CB23 7EN

www.belbin.com

The Belbin Guide to Succeeding at Work

Succeeding at Work...

... is about knowing which role to play
in a given situation.

The Belbin Guide to Succeeding at Work

Introduction

Is becoming well-qualified the key to success in working life? No one would doubt that qualifications help, but perhaps they are not as significant as people think. Many educated individuals (with certificates to prove it) are left pondering on disappointments as their careers proceed but ultimately grind to a halt. For continuing advancement, new skills need to be learned in either management or business.

In employment, the ability to handle people and behave appropriately becomes crucial to career progress at every turn. Some people possess these skills to an outstanding degree so that their rise – often from humble backgrounds – becomes a source of wonder and public comment. Others have started well and have then become frustrated and locked into a position in which they are unhappy. Why are some people more effective in the workplace than others? Is it nurture or nature? Or is it more connected with the way in which jobs are drawn up and how well individuals are matched to their demands?

I hope that this short book will offer some leads. I have long been interested in individual differences in personality. Having been involved in Industrial Psychology for the last 60 years, I have spent much of my time evaluating people's contributions in the workplace. Relationships are always important and, since I wrote *Management Teams: Why They Succeed Or Fail*, back in 1981, people have identified with what has now become well-known as the language of Belbin Team Roles. This has helped numerous individuals determine their own contribution to teams.

In *The Belbin Guide to Succeeding at Work*, the reader is guided through the problems commonly faced in employment. In many management and self-help business books, advice is given uniformly to individuals on how to act and behave, irrespective of their own personal traits. In this book, we try to induce in readers a sense of realism both about themselves and the situations they will encounter. Without this knowledge, nobody is adequately equipped to succeed in the workplace.

To progress in an organisation, an individual needs to have a clear understanding of where to fit in and how best to make a personal contribution. This orientation is not a one-off affair either. It needs to continue throughout the span of working life. It is never too late to learn, and it is always too soon to stop learning. So carry on reading and reflecting. We hope you will enjoy doing so.

Meredith Belbin

CHAPTER ONE

Understanding ourselves, our potential and the situation

If we want to progress and succeed at work we need to understand that it is our behaviour that provides the key. For we will only be given opportunities by our bosses, if we can convince them of our potential. To do that, they must believe that we can come up with appropriate behaviour and excel at what we are required to do. But what does this mean – surely we all know how to behave?

Our behaviour is defined by what we do or say and how we react in any particular situation. It is in essence how we come across to others and it is the basis of how people interact. When we come to reflect on how to behave at work, we need to look beyond the horizons of our usual instinctive behaviour. Work imposes its own demands and we are not there just to give expression to our own personality. After all, we are being paid for what we do.

Our own propensities

Human beings are creatures of habit which in other words means that we are rather predictable in the way we behave. We seem to give few behavioural surprises to others – least of all to the ones who have known us a long time. Perhaps we also find it hard to change how we behave towards those who already have a preconception about our behaviour.

A dilemma

As we proceed through our working lives, we frequently change the way we behave. And yet we still feel we are the same person. So how do we reconcile these differences? Can we be two different things at the same time? The answer is that we can. We adapt our behaviour to fit different situations, often without any sense of conflict. It is just as well that we do. Failing to adjust our behaviour is equivalent to being unresponsive to others. No one adopting that attitude would easily progress in a career or be liked by their fellow beings. So that poses a dilemma. We have to consider how to develop character and grow in maturity without losing a sense of personal identity.

So how do we reconcile the two? Are we all very different characters who have our own idiosyncrasies and set patterns of behaviour or are we chameleons who simply adjust to the situations we find ourselves in? Perhaps the answer is that we are both. The first step in combining the two is to understand ourselves.

Understanding ourselves

We need to understand ourselves in order to gain direction. Over a period of time we begin to build up a sense of the things we like doing and the things we perceive we are good at. We have a comfort zone and if we go too far outside its boundaries we feel a certain amount of stress. Individual differences become apparent at an early age and although no character is set in stone, our own unique behavioural fingerprint begins to show. Some of these clusters of characteristics will become useful in the work place.

Our potential

All through our lives we are continually letting others see how we behave and react in different situations. Every time we have a go at something new, we show others our potential. Normally confidence is gained by success and is diminished by failure, but sometimes our own understanding of ourselves is misplaced. We can become over-confident or under-confident in our own abilities. Over-confidence however can be a handicap. No-one will believe a "know all" or a self proclaimed all-round expert. Those who win the support of others usually come from the range of ordinary mortals. They will be observed to possess some positive strengths along with some admitted weaknesses.

What we need is a reality check from other people – a democratic one and one that does not damage the ego. In this way we can be guided to areas where our own contributions can be best appreciated and used to greatest effect. Further on in the book we will look at how this can be achieved, but first let us look at the nature of work and situations in which we find ourselves.

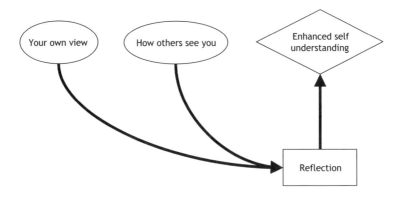

Adapting to the situation

The world of work is continually changing. And if we are to survive and indeed succeed, we need to change too. That entails learning to contribute in more than one way.

Many organisations, private and public, endorse the idea of "competencies." This means that you as a worker should be able to tick as large a number of boxes as possible, hit all desirable targets and be well received by all the people you encounter in your employment. But people don't work in this way. Eventually, natural preferences and dislikes will surface. You will naturally work better with some people than with others. No one is equally competent at all tasks. The good news is that such inequality is no impediment to progress and efficiency. In fact, if we *were* equally competent at all tasks, it would be difficult to decide who should do what or who should work with whom.

The different abilities and inclinations of members of a team provide an insight into the best way of getting things done. In complementary working relationships, individuals can achieve more than they would if they worked alone. In any team formed or any pairing between two individuals, each person will have to consider what they can bring to the party and where they can fit in best.

Employees and managers will naturally gravitate towards the people they like to work with and the type of work that fits in with their personal needs. That is why it is helpful if individuals project their preferences while avoiding the dangers of doing so too emphatically, for jobs contain an obligatory element. Any organisation which fashioned jobs solely in the interests of employees would be heading for bankruptcy. So a balance has to be struck between your needs and those of the organisation.

This division first becomes apparent at interview. In applying for a job there is a need to convey enthusiasm and experience. However, the job in question may not be entirely appropriate for you. This may not be obvious at first, since job titles have a tendency towards the grandiose.

Another common problem is one of uncertainty. What if you don't know exactly what you want to do? No one who wants to secure a job offer can afford to admit such doubts. A more common strategy is to appear versatile and willing regardless, but will this have a detrimental effect on your longer-term goals?

To become a highly-valued employee, you need to think on both fronts. The first need is to become aware of the broad range of demands placed on any organisation; the second need is to assess what part you can best play. But how do you go about making the job your own? And how do you find your feet and make progress if you're not sure where your talents lie?

To those in management, nothing matters more than having the right people in the right positions. This is in fact teamwork at its most effective. You can help with the process by understanding the job, and by understanding yourself.

To summarise:

- Understanding and managing our own behaviour is the key to being appreciated at work.

- We need to adapt our behaviour according to the situation.

- We need to be aware of how we are interacting with others.

- People need to be in positions that suit their talents.

CHAPTER TWO

Jobs and work

Wouldn't it be nice to find the perfect job? Is there really such a job out there that is ideally designed for you? Perhaps it is best looking at the question the other way around. Is there an organisation out there that can use your potential? The answer is yes – but you won't know until you dip your toe in the water. The first thing to do when considering a new job is to look at the job on offer and the nature of the work. Then – if you decide it is right for you – you will have to apply and be accepted.

When you're circling adverts in the newspaper, the grandiose job titles can seem like a far cry from reality. Job titles and descriptions are designed to sell jobs. A Pest Control Officer covers a rat catcher. A Vision Clearance Engineer actually means window cleaning. A Stock Replenishment Advisor is revealed as a supermarket shelf stacker. A Sales Executive denotes seniority, yet the job itself may call for little beyond cold calling on the telephone or doorstep. The term

"Consultant" is an umbrella term for a large number of occupations implying prestige and professionalism. Disappointingly, it will sometimes mean that there is no real job involved. The reality is: "We are prepared to call on you from time to time and if we do you will get paid."

So how do you know what to look for in a job? The ideal is to be offered a job with scope for development into a fulfilling career. Researching your prospective company on the web is a good start. However, this strategy will only get you so far if internal culture and public image don't match. The company website won't necessarily provide you with the details you need to know. You may see the image the company presents to the world, but you won't necessarily get a feel for the place.

You will get the chance to find out what you need to at interview. But the first priority is to come across well. You don't want to ruin your chances before you've found out whether the job is suitable. So how do you behave at interview?

Firstly, enthusiasm counts for a lot. An attractive job will mean lots of competition from other candidates, and you'll want to look like the perfect match for the job, both on paper and in person. This means polishing your CV as well as dry-cleaning your suit.

Getting through the door

Let's not take the basics for granted. Your CV and application form (if there is one) must be devoid of mistakes. You need to arrive on time ("The traffic was terrible" will not do). Your clothes must be appropriate for the occasion and in accord with the expectation of the interviewers ("I always dress like this" is out). Finally, it is always a good thing to have some pre-existing knowledge of the company. That will enable you to ask well-judged questions that will signify your interest. Make sure you know the company's business before you go in, or you're unlikely to impress.

The success of an interview depends on establishing rapport. Therefore you need to prepare something worthwhile to talk about, in case awkward silences arise. Also be prepared to pick up and run with something an interviewer has said. Some interviewers are very poor at interviewing, in which case roles can be exchanged: the interviewee becomes the interviewer. The common mistake is for interviewees to talk too much in the belief that they are impressing. Be concise: say what you want to say, but don't babble.

When it comes to asking questions of your interviewer, don't turn your interview into the Spanish Inquisition: some compromise is needed. Asking questions about the nature of the job will demonstrate your enthusiasm, provided that the questions are formulated in the right way. Asking how late you will have to stay on at work is not going to produce a good impression. A good general rule is to ask questions from genuine interest, not because you feel obliged to do so.

Indicating interests and abilities above and beyond the job will make you stand out from the crowd as an interesting and well-rounded person. It will also give them indications of where you would be best used, which may result in a re-definition of the job before it is offered to you. While the job is in its formative stages, shape it to fit your talents and ambitions as much as possible, as there will probably be less room for manoeuvre later.

The different reasons for working

So you've researched the company and you've established your needs. But how do you know if the interviewer is thinking along the same lines? Don't assume that everyone at the interview has the same priorities as you do. Whilst there are common needs that must be addressed, individual motivations vary enormously.

When it comes to the question of why we work, new patterns are emerging all the time. Taking on a new financial commitment or having a loved one dependent upon you might lead you to rate job security very highly. Others look for challenges: the greater the challenge, the more attractive the job. In other cases, what matters most to applicants is the appropriateness of the job for the skills and qualifications they possess, since they see this as the route towards fulfilment.

The pie chart below shows the results from a sample of 100 managers who took the Belbin Job Feature Questionnaire (JFQ), which investigates what people look for and value in a job. A great number of different reasons for working were identified and then grouped under "job content," "drive" and "lifestyle." These headings were sub-categorised as shown.

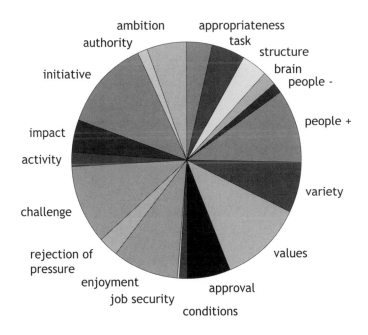

The results within these groups varied tremendously. Initiative, challenge, interaction with others ("people +") and enjoyment were among the highest-rated responses, with job security, seclusion ("people -") and authority among the lowest ranking. Some of the categories are fairly self-explanatory; others are more complex. What is certain is that we all have our own agendas when it comes to work. You can find a full glossary of the terms defined for the purposes of the JFQ at the back of this book.

Your changing needs

Reasons for working are liable to change over time. It is likely that a twenty-year-old will prioritise variety, risk and excitement more than a sixty-year-old will. Priorities in life change with age, need and circumstance. A desire for status could be linked with self-esteem. Determination can be triggered by hunger.

Maslow's Hierarchy of Needs was developed in the 1940s to explain people's motivations. The essential premise is that there are certain needs which must be met before others will be of concern. The chart below illustrates the theory:

Maslow's Hierarchy of Needs

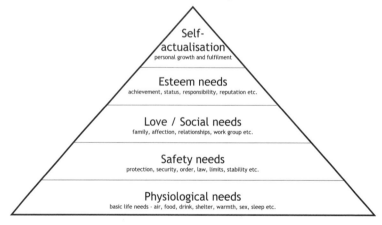

Being aware of these needs is essential to understanding motivations in the workplace. You are hoping that the job will fulfil most of your current needs. On the other side of the equation, the interviewer is hoping that you match expectations and that you fit in with company culture. In summary, a compatible relationship is required between the two parties. Unless this is achieved, the job offer may be short-lived.

To summarise:

- Gain a clear understanding of what is involved in the job.

- Give yourself the best possible chance at interview.

- Understand the motives for work and how your needs change over time.

CHAPTER THREE

Finding Your Role in a Team

So congratulations, the job is yours and you've spent the last few weeks working out who takes sugar in their coffee. It's now time to establish how you and everything you have brought to the job can serve to help the team. You will need to find a happy co-existence with your work colleagues. Some you may care for more than others, but nevertheless productive working relationships need to be formed. The main tool you have at your disposal is language, but why doesn't this always seem to work out?

Although communication is crucial, the language we use at work is often prone to ambiguity and misinterpretation, which can unwittingly cause offence, or simply confuse. Comments about others can be subjective, simplistic and unhelpful when it is necessary to promote an effective work environment. Instead, a common, meaningful language is required to bridge the gap between ourselves and our colleagues.

A long-running experiment

A unique study of teams took place at Henley Management College in the 1970s. The question posed was "What makes some teams succeed, and others fail?" The upshot was a ten-year period of observational research using a simulation.

The simulation was a management game designed at Henley to reproduce work life. It contained all the principal variables that typify the problems of decision-making in a business environment. The experiment was designed along scientific lines with careful measurement at each stage. Those participating were invited to take psychometric tests, plus a test of high level reasoning ability (called the Critical Thinking Appraisal). Teams of various designs were composed on the basis of these individual test scores. Every half-minute, the contribution of the person speaking was recorded and classified into one of seven categories by trained observers. At the end of the exercise, which ran off and on throughout a week, the results of each team (operating as a company) were presented financially, which allowed more effective and less effective "companies" to be compared.

What was at first deemed to be likely was that high-intellect teams would succeed where lower-intellect teams would not. However, the outcome of this research was that certain teams, predicted to be excellent based on intellect, failed to fulfil their potential.

In fact, it became apparent by looking at the various combinations that it was not intellect, but *balance*, which

The Belbin Guide to Succeeding at Work

enabled a team to succeed. Successful "companies" were characterised by the compatibility of the roles that their members played while unsuccessful companies were subject to role conflict. Using information from psychometric tests and the CTA, predictions could be made on the roles that individuals played and ultimately on whether the company would be more likely to figure among the winners or losers.

One interesting point to observe from the experiment was that individuals reacted very differently within the same broad situation. It is a common experience that individual differences can cause a group to fall apart. People just don't fit in. On the other hand, variation in personal characteristics can become a source of strength if they are recognised and taken into account. So understanding the nature of these differences can become an essential first step in the management of people, providing one can recognise what is useful for a given situation and what is not.

The most successful companies tended to be those with a mix of different people, i.e. those with a range of different behaviours. In fact, eight distinct clusters of behaviour turned out to be distinctive and useful. These were called "Team Roles," and in fact, a ninth based on specialist knowledge was to emerge later. These Team Roles have been used in organisations and teams across the world ever since. They have been immensely useful in making teams more effective. Most important is the way they can be of great use to you as a working individual. It is up to you to decide which roles to play and which to avoid.

A Team Role was defined as a *tendency to behave, contribute and interrelate with others in a particular way.* The following are the nine Team Roles, and how you will recognise each one.

Plant

Plants are imaginative and unorthodox.

"Webb Ellis, stop – that's not in the rules!"

Plants generate initial ideas. Plants are so called for historical reasons. In the management exercise, it was discovered that there was no initial spark unless a creative individual was "planted" in each company, so giving each a chance of success. Good ideas are always valuable when problems are complex.

In an office, Plants are easy to pick out. They are unconventional in their thinking, providing imaginative and original lines of thought when the team is stuck for ideas. They are there to offer the vital "eureka!" moments, and as is the nature of such thought-processes, they are frequently up-in-the-clouds as they examine things in their own particular way. Such time spent in off-the-wall thinking is needed. In order to recognise their full potential, Plants need a position where they are allowed to be creative, producing ideas like welcome fruit to be harvested by others in the team.

So, for a person to be a true Plant, they must have a creative disposition and be able to think laterally. This kind of behaviour is not always appreciated in structured organisations, however, as it tends to rock the boat. Yet it is the Plant who can offer the seed of an idea which leads to greater things, and without that seed, a team will stagnate. This said, the other extreme can cause a different kind of stalemate. With too many Plants in the mix, liaison and co-operation will be severely limited, with each off in their own little world.

Monitor Evaluator

Monitor Evaluators are logical, discriminating
and always make the right decision.

The Monitor Evaluator is a very logical, analytical being –
typically a high performer on the Watson-Glaser *Critical
Thinking Appraisal*, which was one of the tests used at Henley
to identify different abilities. Monitor Evaluators will take the
ideas of a Plant and subject them to the most intense
scrutiny, taking into account all facets in an unemotional
way. Sometimes over-critical, frequently sceptical, they
nevertheless provide a reasoned mind that curbs excessive
enthusiasm. Without a Monitor Evaluator to put a rein on

the Plant, the most ridiculous ideas might be allowed to go further than they should, wasting time and money.

Monitor Evaluators are represented by the Belbin icon as an all-seeing eye. Spatially, we often think of them as positioned slightly outside the group. This is not to say that they are isolated. They are likely to be the first to be called upon whenever a discerning view is needed. What they possess, however, is sufficient emotional detachment to prevent their judgement from becoming clouded.

A good Monitor Evaluator knows when criticism is appropriate. Here is a neat test of any Monitor Evaluator. If your enthusiastic cry of: "I have an idea..." is received with thoughtful nodding, then ten tough questions on how it will work, how much it will cost and whether it has already been done, they're doing the required job as a Monitor Evaluator. On the other hand, if your suggestion is met with: "NO! NO! IT WON'T WORK, I TELL YOU, IT WON'T WORK!" before you're through the door, you're dealing with a pessimist rather than a Monitor Evaluator. The difference? A Monitor Evaluator builds their scepticism on logic; a pessimist doesn't.

A mature Plant will welcome the criticism of a good Monitor Evaluator and modify a proposed strategy. But it can be a sensitive meeting of attitudes. When the Plant's originality meets the inalienable logic of the Monitor Evaluator, sparks are likely to fly. Then it's time for some mediation.

Co-ordinator

Co-ordinators clarify goals, promote decision making and involve others in appropriate ways.

The Co-ordinator excels in getting the best from any team of people, which is why what is needed is a mature, confident individual, who will spread a feeling of calm around the group. Regardless of rank, Co-ordinators are naturally suited to chairing meetings, because of their capacity to manage and develop other members of the team. Because they are able to identify others' talents, Co-ordinators possess skills at delegating work and choosing the most suitable team member to take on a particular task or responsibility. In a meeting or discussion, they make sure that everyone is given a chance to make their contribution. If a Plant is struggling to explain a new idea, and the Monitor Evaluator is proving overly dismissive, the Co-ordinator will hopefully step in to facilitate communication and progress between the two.

The Plant, Monitor Evaluator and Co-ordinator could happily work as a small unit, generating and vetting ideas in a co-operative and constructive way. But this unit would be unproductive, since none of them actually do any work! Enter the Implementer, someone who's focused on the task, and to whom the Co-ordinator can entrust the organisation and follow-through of the project.

Implementer

Implementers are disciplined, systematic
and love structure.

So nobody is getting on and doing anything. Sound familiar?
This is when the diligence and the methodical approach of
the Implementer proves welcome. Perhaps not the
highest-profile member of the team, this is a hard-working
individual, without whose efforts the team's ideas would go
nowhere. It is commonly observed that people choose the bits
of work they like doing and ignore the rest. Not so for the
Implementer, who will do what needs to be done for the good
of the company.

The Belbin icon for this Team Role is a cog: an essential part of the infrastructure or organisation; someone who gets things moving and then keeps the ball rolling. Unlike the scatty Plant, this person's desk is likely to be organised, with everything filed methodically by size and colour.

There is, however, a price to be paid. Once you've got a cog moving, the process of trying to make it move in another direction is difficult. Implementers are most comfortable working with reliable, effective processes which produce good results. Shaking things up and doing things differently will inevitably interrupt this efficiency at an operational level, and this can make the Implementer slow to respond to change, or even resistant to it altogether.

Completer Finisher

Completer Finishers are anxious people, who worry about standards and detail. They perfect...

"Give it a fourth coat Donavan, just in case..."

Need to find a needle in a haystack? That is the challenge to which your resident Completer Finisher is well placed to respond. Here's another Team Role to be found hard at work. Completer Finishers are painstakingly meticulous, investing their close attention and bringing their love of accuracy to bear on every detail of a plan, product or report. They'll act as quality control – editing, checking and re-checking until they are completely satisfied with the final outcome. The irony about the Completer Finisher is that they can be so obsessed with quality that they fail to finish in time. They polish rather than finish.

A copy editor is highly likely to be a Completer Finisher, or you'll find it somewhere prominent in their Team Role profile. Whereas creative Team Roles might lose interest after they have penned the article and brought the initial idea to fruition, Completer Finishers see the job as just beginning. They will make sure that any spelling or grammatical errors have been removed, and that all the nuts and bolts of the operation have been correctly tightened.

It is important to realise, when you're dealing with Completer Finishers, that their behaviours are often driven by anxiety, even when this might be masked. The Completer Finisher will worry until a satisfactory result has been achieved and deadlines met. Anxiety is the opposite of complacency, so you can be sure your Completer Finisher won't be a cocky, *laissez-faire* person. The tendency to check and double check, however, comes at a cost. That cost is to be obsessive, coupled with a reluctance to delegate work to others. This may result in an overloaded Completer Finisher who is likely to fall victim to stress unless protected by others in the team.

So you have a finished product: created by the Plant, examined by the Monitor Evaluator, produced by the Implementer and checked by the Completer Finisher, with the Co-ordinator ensuring that the team is working and communicating well, and that they are listening to one another.

But what are your competitors up to? Could you be buying your materials more cheaply? How are you going to market the product? Can you seek advice from someone who has managed a similar project before? With only the Team Roles we have discussed so far, the team would be at risk of becoming very insular. What is needed is someone who is willing to branch out and look outside the team for information and ideas.

Resource Investigator

Resource Investigators are enthusiastic, inquisitive and explore opportunities.

If the Plant is the initial "eureka!" light bulb, the Resource Investigator is more like a sack marked "SWAG." What the Plant creates within one organisation, the Resource Investigator will borrow and improve from another. The striking thing about Resource Investigators is their bold and outgoing nature, countering the Monitor Evaluator's pessimism with optimism. The downside of this optimism is that, like the Plant, they risk being euphoric and failing to follow through, losing interest and becoming bored quickly.

Yet Resource Investigators are greatly valued for their ability to attract new business with their energy and enthusiasm. They possess an inquisitive nature. Not only are they good at finding out about where to source a necessary item, they also have persuasive skills which can be ideal for selling. Studies have shown that Resource Investigators are more successful than other Team Roles in gaining job offers. They are also quite effective being self-employed as they source the market and spot opportunities. Resource Investigators are sometimes described as *"rarely in the office and always on the phone when they are."*

The other side of enthusiasm can be boredom and this is why Resource Investigators sometimes need to be prodded in order to continue the momentum that otherwise may fade and die. Delivery can be their downside, so this is an area where they need to rely on others.

Shaper

Shapers are dynamic and make things happen.

"Excuse me! The soup is cold. Can you get everyone a new one?"

When it comes to reaching a goal, Shapers will get you there. Quickly. Shapers are often admired for the way they manage to get things done and succeed in getting people moving, but their tactics for doing this are not always welcome. They're extroverts, like Resource Investigators, but more highly-strung. Being no-nonsense individuals they are not afraid to be blunt.

One of the most useful things a Shaper brings to a team is the great injection of energy and urgency. Shapers make their mark because they are achievers and are determined to find a way round any obstacle and bring others with them. Their downside is that they often come across as aggressive. Too many Shapers will be disruptive and are liable to clash explosively with one another. Shapers need to be thinly-spread. If they are not careful they can win the battle and lose the war. They need an ally to work with who diffuses tension.

Teamworker

Teamworkers are diplomatic, popular and
avert friction.

*Wherever he went, Frank managed to improve the
atmosphere...*

Enter the Teamworker, the most diplomatic and sensitive
member of the team. If you've just been offended by your
resident Shaper, or had your Co-ordinator load work at your
door, the Teamworker is the person who will make you feel
better about it. A Teamworker makes sure everyone is
comfortable, lightens the atmosphere, and provides an
empathetic, listening ear. They use intuition to promote a
good atmosphere. A good Teamworker is likely to be a
popular member of the team. As well as caring deeply about

their colleagues and the team as a whole, they offer versatility and diplomacy. When the Shaper rubs the team up the wrong way, the Teamworker can act as a foil, cementing good relationships between colleagues and taking on the work that needs to be done.

The downside to this is that because Teamworkers are keen to please, they can fail to impart reality when news is bad. This can also lead to indecisiveness when a course of action might upset others.

The ninth Team Role

In the original experimental studies at Henley, prior knowledge and experience had no part to play in the management exercise that had been designed. No team therefore enjoyed any starting advantage in the exercise. In practice such a situation is entirely artificial. Every project needs to start from somewhere, which means getting someone involved who knows a lot about the subject. By nature, a specialist is someone prepared continually to expand and develop knowledge in a particular area in order to become an expert in his or her field. As Specialist is a Team Role we spell it with a capital letter.

Specialist

Specialists are professionally dedicated, single-minded and are prepared to build up their knowledge.

Because the word "specialist" is already in common usage, the Specialist tends to be the most misunderstood Team Role of all. The key thing to remember about the Specialist is that – in Team Role terms at least – it is a way of behaving just like any other Team Role, and not a job title. It therefore doesn't mean someone with a particular academic or technical background.

A Specialist in this new sense is a self-reliant individual dedicated to an area of expertise – a real fount of knowledge determined to know absolutely everything there is to know about a particular topic.

Leaving the workplace for a moment, it might be easy to think of examples of this type of behaviour in everyday life. The Specialist is the kind of person who, on purchasing a new mobile phone or DVD player, reads the product manual from start to finish in order to discover how to use all of its various functions. The Specialist displays a thirst for knowledge – an attribute which makes this individual invaluable in many situations. A Specialist does not necessarily denote someone who has had a particular academic or technical education. Remember, the subject of Team Roles deals with natural behaviour, not credentials.

Technical knowledge and interest are invaluable qualities in the right place. But too much of it soon becomes off-putting to others who don't share the same fascination with the subject. Loss of interest becomes difficult to disguise, and yet you will commonly find that the Specialist will take no notice but carry on as before.

Find out your Team Roles

All nine Team Roles have now been covered. A mix of these roles is needed in every organisation if it is to work well. Each of these roles can be of value in the right place. What is important is that every team member becomes a good example of a preferred type.

We have also established that each role comes with its strengths and weaknesses. These weaknesses need not always present a problem. Provided they are recognised and admitted, they can be balanced by a Team Role strength in another.

If you wish to make the most of yourself at work and be at your most effective, then you will need to identify your personal set of Team Role strengths. We all have our own combination of top roles. This fingerprint will underlie your own particular work style.

Measure yourself through self and observers: Why the perception of others matter

Team Roles focus on behaviours. If our interest were confined to personality, it could be argued that no one else could know or understand you better than you know yourself.

With behaviour, however, it's a different story. Whilst you might think you are sending out a certain message, other people might read your actions and words very differently, and in that case, it's important to know. Whilst your self-perception can tell you what you think of yourself, and what your aspirations might be, simply relying on your own perception of your behaviour is unlikely to improve self-awareness (and won't prove as interesting!)

What matters in the workplace is what your managers, colleagues and subordinates think of you, since you are likely to be assigned tasks on that basis. For a broader view of how you really are, and how others see you, Observer Assessments are desirable. They can indicate how others view you. They can help modify your overall Team Roles to give a more accurate picture of how you come across in the workplace – in short, how you behave at work.

To summarise:

- There are a finite number of behaviours which are useful to a team.

- You should try to understand how each of these roles fit the overall need.

- Find out your own Team Role preferences.

- Get feedback from others for a reality check.

CHAPTER FOUR

Learning to Manage Your Profile

Of course, nothing is definitive in searching for your Team Roles. People have dispositions and propensities. To assume you can get an exact measurement which stays the same for your lifetime is ridiculous. Equally it is just as ridiculous to suggest you can adapt and play the part of each role to the same high standard. Why? Because we have genetic and other influences that distinguish us and make us who we are.

So what is important is to take on a role that suits you. Furthermore you will need to adapt your role according to the situation and who else is in the team. In that way you will be taking on the appropriate role. It is important in life not to decide simply whether you should be a sheep or a wolf, but when to take on either part.

Project Your Image

Success at work is about being recognised for your behavioural contribution. If you want to succeed at work you will need to project your image: your unique combination of Team Role strengths. If you project this well, your manager or work colleagues can use your talents appropriately.

One way of gaining recognition is to learn some favourite phrases in order to project yourself and reinforce your image. The guideline is to gravitate towards the things you do well and to keep your distance from what you do badly, or from things which are better done by others. This simple formula will get you noticed and allow you to get the work that suits your disposition. It ensures the use of the right talents in the right place at the right time.

If you've got it, flaunt it

Accepting what your Team Roles are and how your strengths manifest themselves can be something of a relief. But don't rest on your laurels. Now that you have a clearer idea of what your strengths are, begin to make sure that other people know about them. When you have excelled at a particular piece of work, express satisfaction and a sense of enjoyment. Being voluble about what you enjoy is kind not only to yourself, but also to your employer. It flags up the sort of work they can be happy giving to you, safe in the knowledge that it will be done well. Leaving them to work this out on their own is going to be harder for both of you.

Evidently, no manager is going to be impressed by somebody who just talks the talk, and doesn't walk the walk. But if you express a particular interest or ability in a certain area, and stake your claim for that type of work, then allowing your actions to support your words will be noticed and will earn you respect.

Projecting yourself as you really are has certain advantages. For a start, others will know what to expect. As a result, the right work is more likely to come your way. By establishing a strong identity you could already be on the road to success. The problem is that such a strategy entails risks. What happens when your own strengths overlap with those of another? Two people with independent views and creative ideas seldom form a mutual admiration society. Two people who like organising are better kept apart. By understanding the natural Team Roles of your working associates you are unlikely to commit the mistake of invading another's personal territory.

Team Role sacrifices

The strategy of playing to your strengths and managing your weaknesses by forming complementary partnerships works well in an ideal situation. Unfortunately such situations do not come along as frequently as might be desired. In many teams there are conspicuous gaps. Such gaps have not arisen haphazardly. Many firms have a preference for recruiting individuals of a particular type. That outcome tends to produce uniformity and is the inevitable consequence of a policy known as "cloning." When there is no one to take on an essential role, the options are much reduced because many of the team members will be equally lacking. At this point, somebody needs to make a sacrifice and perform a function that does not come naturally.

Those who understand Team Roles are alert to this need and can prepare themselves to step into the breach. Consider a situation in which a meeting has been concluded but no one has recorded the decisions reached. There is always a feeling of: "That is not my job." But if it is no one's job, the decisions reached will be null and void. The meeting might just as well not have taken place. A sense of duty can impel a person to realise the problem and take on what no one else will do.

Duty is not the only factor. Required action involves both taking account of situational needs and mimicking the form of behaviour that could be expected from someone in the ideal Team Role. To perform the prescribed role well a certain amount of acting is called for. Can you play the part? If you can, a range of opportunities opens up. Playing the role successfully will immediately lead to being recognised as possessing "versatility," an attribute widely appreciated.

Learning to make Team Role sacrifices now becomes a desirable option. But anyone taking on a sacrifice is bound to have reservations. Principally, "How long am I going to stay in a situation out of line with my natural strengths and inclinations?" Such silent questions usually go unanswered. They surface in behavioural ways that surprise and sometimes shock people. The most extreme is that a valued employee leaves to take up another job when there is no obvious financial explanation. The real reason behind this is that a satisfactory performance has been achieved only at a high personal cost. There are no costs in doing what is natural, but there are obvious limits to how long one can endure what one finds stressful.

Learning to make a Team Role sacrifice can have special value in serving the greater good of the team. Nevertheless it should always be seen as a temporary measure. If there are too many Team Role sacrifices, someone is failing to put people together in the right way. Getting the balance right is the key requirement. This is more likely to be achieved if people are performing in a role which comes naturally.

Becoming a good example of the type

Taking on board your predominant Team Roles and cashing in on your strengths will take you a long way. But being a Monitor Evaluator is one thing: being a *good* Monitor Evaluator is another. Unless you can be the latter there is no sense in trying to play the role. For every Team Role you wish to play, there are things that you should strive for, and other things you should avoid in order to become the best possible example of that role. Obviously, if you have decided what your combination of roles might be, then you will need to take on board the dos and don'ts for all of your particular Team Roles. Here are some suggestions…

If you are a Plant...

Do use your creativity to spark off new ideas or think up solutions to problems. Instead of looking at everything as the rest of the team does, try to think round corners to come up with original responses. Use your particular slant to bring a refreshing new angle to things, and try to communicate your ideas simply to your team.

Don't be tempted to evaluate your own ideas for usefulness: this should be left to other team members. Resist the temptation to be possessive over your ideas, too. Co-operation with others is usually a better way forwards. Remember that the team has to come first, and your pride second, in order to lead to real success. Being the only survivor of a ship that has sunk is less use than making it to port.

If you are a Resource Investigator...

Do look beyond the group and go outside its limits in order to create new contacts. You should look for new markets which others in your team may not be aware of, and develop the ideas of the Plants in your team to make them marketable. Use your great energy and optimism to stir up enthusiasm in others.

Don't let the team down by neglecting to follow up on things you have arranged. There is no point in building up relationships with important clients only to let them down at the crucial moment. Avoid talking too much, to the detriment of others. Remember that there will be some people in your team who will not come forwards at first, but will have to be drawn out. They may have things of real value to contribute, but not enough confidence to air them, particularly when they have to battle with a stream of non-stop verbiage.

If you are a Co-ordinator...

Do use your calm nature and maturity to establish an air of authority and to bring others into discussions when you think they can usefully contribute. Since you are good at acknowledging and balancing the roles of others in your team, prevent any Shapers from being too dominant, and allow others to take the floor. Use praise and encouragement to hold the group together and spur it along.

Don't take credit for what the team accomplishes as a whole, as this will cause resentment. Nor should you try to lay claim to supreme status, or try to delegate your fair share of the work by manipulating others. You will lose your ability to direct people if they feel that you are using them badly or failing to pull your weight.

If you are a Shaper...

Do get things moving. Use your energy and drive to press others and prevent any complacency or laziness in the team. Take advantage of your natural honesty and be straightforward and open with others, so that they know where they stand. Push things forward to make sure your team is achieving all of its goals and hitting deadlines.

Don't hold grudges or become overbearing. Try not to get into a mindset where you feel that deliberately upsetting others is a virtue, and make sure you hold onto your sense of humour when the going gets tough. If you find yourself reprimanding others for unsuitable behaviour, the criticism will be taken in far better humour if you can be good-natured about it.

If you are a Monitor Evaluator...

Do provide your team with a balanced opinion on all ideas and options. Remain objective and use your analytical skills as much as you can. Make sure that you are ready to explain and justify your decisions so that you are not accused of pessimism, and accept questioning with good grace. Even if you feel rushed by a Shaper in your team, take the time you need when making decisions – this will prevent misjudgements and mistakes from occurring.

Don't be critical to the point where you are disliked. If you are cynical without providing logical reasons for being so, people will not respect your opinions. Stop yourself from giving an immediately negative reaction to everything that you hear, simply because you feel rushed. You should be aiming to use your strategic mind to prevent hasty mistakes, not to quash the enthusiasm and drive of the team.

If you are a Teamworker...

Do try to promote a good team atmosphere by reacting to the needs of others. Use your versatile working style to provide support to other team members when necessary, and defuse any hostility that might arise from conflicts. You will find that you can use your popularity to win support for your ideas when needed.

Don't side with the most dominant person to avoid a conflict, or shy away from situations which involve pressure. More important issues will need your input at times and you should be ready to offer it. Remember that decisions ultimately have to be made and lived with, and that you will occasionally have to sacrifice your short-term comfort for the longer-term objective.

If you are an Implementer...

Do create systems for the team which promote organisation and efficiency, and then make sure that you and your colleagues follow them. Use your practical mindset to get down to what needs to be done, especially in terms of turning ideas into action so that they can actually work. If you can, let everyone see that you are more hard-working than others, so that standards and goals are set for everyone else. Show loyalty to your company at all times.

Don't stand in the way of change. New ideas are necessary, so don't be obstructive for the sake of it. Sometimes there will be temporary lapses in efficiency while new structures are put in place. Remember that your work would never have existed if such changes hadn't occurred at some point. Beware of using expressions like, "If it ain't broke, don't fix it", as an excuse to resist change. You may find it difficult, but you will come to adapt along with everyone else, and wonder how anything could ever have been otherwise.

If you are a Completer Finisher...

Do try to raise standards in everything you do. Use your ability to help other members of the team who may not be so strong on accuracy. Make sure that you or other team members follow tasks through to completion. For the company to achieve excellence, attention to detail will be needed at some point in the process, so help the team to achieve this.

Don't allow your perfectionism to become obsessive. At the end of the day, deadlines must be met, and priority has to be given to these. Don't feel that you have to do everything. Others, less set on perfection, can still do their fair share and you should be ready to delegate work if necessary. Resist the temptation to penny pinch or split hairs on trivial issues, or you will lose the support of your colleagues when it really matters.

If you are a Specialist...

Do show your enthusiasm for your particular subject or subjects. Cultivate a sense of real professionalism and encourage your fellow team members to trust your knowledge. Make sure that you keep your knowledge and skills up to date, using training courses if necessary.

Don't inundate people with information when they have asked for something simple. This will only frustrate and confuse them. Avoid being dismissive of factors outside your own area of expertise. Remember that things you have no knowledge of can impinge hugely on you in all areas of life. Also, do not become over-protective of your area. Denying access to others will not help anybody in the long run.

You will notice that, for every Team Role, there are strengths to be cultivated and corresponding weaknesses to be managed. There are no universal "dos" and "don'ts," and you will probably recognise some of the behaviours and not others. The more you can show your Team Role strengths without displaying the relative weaknesses, the better an example of the type you will become.

To summarise:

- Let people know who you are.

- Be prepared to take on other roles for the good of the team.

- Focus on excelling in those areas for which you have an affinity.

CHAPTER FIVE

How to Handle Difficult People

Difficult situations versus difficult people

We all have difficulties at work. In managing these, the first question to ask is whether problems experienced are due to personal preferences or reflect wider organisational shortcomings. Dealing with a failing infrastructure requires a different approach from dealing with a difficult person or those who are not performing to a high enough professional standard. Singling out an individual when the organisation is to blame merely compounds the problem and diverts attention from the real cause.

Who exactly is difficult?

Wherever sizeable numbers of people come together, almost certainly someone will have earned the reputation of being "a difficult person." However, that does not mean that everyone will find that person difficult. But almost certainly the difficulty will have causes and the causes need to be understood. Any employee who can handle a "difficult person" will be greatly valued.

Awkward pairings

Personal factors figure very strongly in some situations. Clashes of personality occur when two people have divergent approaches. Here opposite Team Role patterns might provide a clue to the problem. A Resource Investigator will be fast-moving and outward-looking, while a Completer Finisher will be inward-looking and reluctant to leave an item of work until a given goal has been satisfactorily met. Mutual irritation is the likely result. So also, a Plant thrives on new ideas while an Implementer is more concerned with practical factors. In both cases there is scope for these diverse characters to work together, provided that each understands and values the role of the other. Problems can be caused when they fail to respect a different style of contribution. Finding a common goal will allow both characters to play their distinct parts.

If a common objective and mutual respect can't be found, then this pairing is unlikely to work. It would therefore be best for these individuals to be kept apart, regardless of their personal talents.

Coping with moderately difficult people

Certain individuals are difficult in the eyes of some. But there are others who seem to be able to work well with them. The difference is that the latter are more skilled in adapting their behaviour to suit the particular person.

If you find yourself in conflict with someone difficult, ask yourself: is this behaviour justified? Has it been prompted by my words or actions? Would their behaviour change if I reacted in a different way?

Success in handling difficult people depends on being able to draw on a range of approaches. A successful salesperson understands this, and can adapt to maximise the outcome of the relationship. Those who learn to adapt to their customers often achieve a successful rapport. If the person on the other end of the phone is cautious and questioning, it would be foolhardy to rush them into a decision. Conversely, if someone's time is limited, and they need to get to the crux of the matter as quickly as possible, it wouldn't make sense to dwell on technicalities.

In extreme cases, people may be considered difficult. They are difficult because they stretch others too far to work effectively with them. However, it is still possible to find a way forward by treating others as they would wish to be treated, not as you would wish to be treated yourself.

Too many people occupying the same ground

Some types of difficulty are functions not of the personality but of the work situation in which two or more people find themselves. People can appear to be difficult because their objectives conflict. A machine operator may have a production target, while an inspector is there to ensure that quality standards are met. The prime aim of an estate agent will be to talk up the merits of a house, while the client's surveyor will look for building faults – often with a view to pulling down the selling-price. Neither party is likely to be impressed with the other's arguments. That does not mean both individuals are difficult, only that the two parties are embroiled in a difficult situation. The recommendation is that when a conflict of interest separates two parties, the argument should never become personal. Only by depersonalising the situation is a compromise ever likely to be found.

*"Personally... I find your attitude
aggressive and offensive..."*

Problems often arise not because people differ but because they are too much alike. They share the same interests, possess similar talents and take the same approach. The result is that they fall over each other, have difficulty in establishing personal identity and fail to gain the potential advantages of symbiosis. They feel uncomfortable but have no grounds for complaint.

Human society has developed by building on diversity through the division of labour. The larger the social or communal unit, the finer this division of labour needs to become. An undifferentiated mass can never be productive. Creating different jobs, where these are clearly defined, provides one means of coping with the problem. But where people share work, natural differences in Team Roles can solve the problem of identity while adding to their productive synergy.

Teams need to learn the language of Team Roles to enable them to work co-operatively, while retaining their individuality and natural aptitudes. For example, a Co-ordinator and a Shaper struggling for dominance in a project may appreciate each other's approaches when articulated in Team Role language. Without this shared language, the risk of making an unhelpful personal attack is greater. Learning to use the key Team Role concepts in a flexible way is essential for developing the skills that make for good teamwork.

Bureaucratic sources of trouble

Even for those of us fortunate enough not to work directly for a bureaucratic institution, there will be times in working life when such establishments have to be encountered. The task of sidestepping frustrating processes and working the system can seem daunting, if not impossible. But understanding the nature of organisations steeped in red tape will help you to find your way.

When institutions become depersonalised, it is an unfortunate fact that their employed personnel bear the brunt of the blame. Their duties have to be performed with little or no protection or support. Ironically, those who work in a failing system are more aware than anyone of the faults and can see the needed remedies. However, they may not be in a position to make drastic changes, and risk being perceived as disloyal if they try.

If you are working in or with a bureaucracy, you can actually bring about change. To ensure that you are not seen as disloyal, it is important to show tolerance and patience in dealing with the red tape, and not to expect changes overnight. Instead, take account of how seemingly difficult people are likely to have been briefed. Do not be tempted to shoot the messenger. Where possible, secure them as allies instead. Those within a system often know the best routes for getting round stumbling blocks and will readily offer unofficial advice if treated with sympathy.

Impossible relationships

It would seem from these previous examples that the onus falls on you to adapt and deal with seemingly difficult people in the appropriate way with diplomacy and discretion. On the other hand, none of these examples can disguise the fact that some individuals would be liabilities in any organisation. They may be too self-centred to work with others, or lazy, incompetent and bad-tempered. They are a burden weighing heavily on both customers and colleagues. It would be a mistake to spend too much time and energy trying to reform them or attempting to harness the relationship. If you are the manager of such an employee, you should take on board that the interests of difficult employees should never be placed above those of the wider corporate body and its stakeholders.

These cases are fortunately few. But where real people problems occur, they should be recognised for what they are and discussed in terms of the options legitimately open and humanly reasonable. In fact, a lot can be done to avoid such situations beforehand. Getting the right person into the right job in the first place is a better solution than treating a complex personnel crisis.

To summarise:

- Analyse how and why the difficult situation has arisen.

- Consider what effect your own behaviour is having on the problem.

- Work out what you need to do to improve the chemistry.

- Check whether the root of the problem is connected with the balance of the team.

CHAPTER SIX

"The Way We Do Things Round Here": Organisational Culture

Different forms of organisation

Institutions, state political systems and international bodies all have their own cultures. Sometimes, these cultures are predetermined by their values and beliefs rather than by any procedural matter. Alternatively, they may have been imposed on their members over a long period of time.

Think of culture as the identity of a company. Any corporate body has to define itself, both to those within and without the organisation. Companies establish values and practices to which employees can relate and refer. Useful and profitable behaviours are rewarded; unhelpful or inappropriate ones are excluded.

To provide structure, a culture must exclude something. Otherwise, it would simply be a confused collection of employees' values, which would make for a shapeless organisation with little or no direction. People often talk casually of a company's "values", when what they really mean is "priorities" or "objectives." Individuals may feel that their work sits well with their personal values, or that the two are in conflict. In many ways, this is a side issue. It is more crucial that employees understand the operational features of an organisation and how it impacts on relations with the outside world.

Externally, organisations strive to present a business front or corporate identity: a kind of "shop window" to competitors, clients and investors, which summarises what they stand for and how they operate. Vast sums of money are spent in developing this identity: mission and vision statements, brands, logos and even merchandise. This is simply a way of marking out an identity for the organisation: defining its boundaries and promoting a positive image.

"I hope you progress up the company ladder Miss Jones"

New individuals coming into this organisation will initially identify with the external image, but must eventually adapt to fit the internal culture.

However, it may not be that simple. Your path to progress may be barred by prejudices regardless of your own behaviour and personal merit. However, we are going to concentrate on those large numbers of organisations with hierarchies based on performance. Your behaviour in such organisations will have a direct bearing on your progress.

How to behave as a new employee

A challenge awaits anyone entering a new organisation or department. What goes on around here? How do people behave? How do they dress? What is permitted? What should employees avoid? Usually no one steps forward to pass on that information. If you're one of the lucky ones, you may be asked to attend an introductory training course where all is revealed, but such a system is rare. It is more likely that you'll have to find your own bearings.

Custom and practice vary from one place to another, even between different parts of the same company situated in different locations. How does a newcomer know what to expect? One solution is to observe. How long do people take for lunch? Are you supposed to offer everyone a cup of tea or just make your own? Are you expected to abide by a particular email etiquette?

Another solution is to seek guidance. Asking pertinent questions shows that you understand the way things are supposed to be done and are willing to acclimatise.

Whether conscious of it or not, most people adapt to the evident culture at work, recognising what is acceptable and unacceptable. Some do so more capably than others. In some instances, what is required of you is made plain. In other companies, it's a case of osmosis, so don't expect anything overnight. The fact of the matter is that, wherever people find themselves, they are expected to fit in with their surroundings.

Avoiding the pitfalls of culture conflicts

Culture conflicts are common where an organisation functions as lots of autonomous departments. Production tends to like long, uninterrupted runs, whereas financial departments favour keeping costs down by holding the minimum of "work in process." These differing objectives affect the culture of a company, which may periodically shift to reflect the relative power of different departments. The successful employee will have learned to act as a diplomat.

Politics has been defined as "the art of the possible." So also, "the art of the possible" holds an important position in many complex employment situations. There is seldom an ideal solution – more often one that fits a particular situation at a particular time. A useful formula for behaving well at work is "to tread softly but with purpose."

Team Roles and culture

Once the successes of a particular individual or group are known, it is tempting to try and reproduce those characteristics which are seen to have brought the company success. The attributes of a particular employee or group are then taken further, to the organisation at large. They are hailed as invaluable to the company's culture, and become integral to recruitment processes, which are then set up to identify and select particular Team Roles. Very soon, the organisation has a cloned culture, with everyone taking the same approach. Not only will the company discover that it is deficient in other roles, but also, as cracks start to appear, the weaknesses of the dominant Team Role are likely to become more and more pronounced.

Organisations will develop in a particular way, according to the types of person they prefer to recruit. Like chooses like. Hence some cultures are dominated by a particular Team Role type.

A Teamworker might be the model employee in an easy-going company where attention is paid to the atmosphere at work. With concern to ensure that everyone gels, conflict is avoided almost at all costs.

Contrastingly, Shapers are likely to be competitive. If an organisation continues to recruit Shapers (and only Shapers) on the basis that they are hard-driving, high-profile and successful individuals, they are likely to end up with a culture plagued by internal conflict. If other Team Roles exist within the organisation, they will be neglected or overwhelmed. Shapers are used to calling the shots and nothing stirs them more than the presence of other Shapers. Because other Team Roles barely figure, there is no teamwork and complications multiply.

With too many Co-ordinators, a different situation will prevail. Impressed by an interviewee's broad perspective and maturity, managers may unwittingly recruit a surfeit of Co-ordinators, each vying to play the same role. At worst, the culture will be a manipulative one, with each person trying to persuade colleagues into doing their bidding. With Co-ordinators being natural delegators, productivity is likely to be low, with everyone trying to limit their own workload. The fallout is liable to cause resentment among those forced to take on more than their fair share. Any Implementers present will be reluctant to put their shoulder to the wheel when others are quick to take the credit for accomplishments. With the vast majority of Co-ordinators favouring a broad outlook, details may fall by the wayside, as specialised knowledge is rejected in favour of generalisations.

A culture of criticism, or even cynicism, can often be attributed to an excessive number of Monitor Evaluators in an organisation. Like the maturity of the Co-ordinator, the logical, analytical brain of the Monitor Evaluator might prove a promising attribute at interview. However, cloning Monitor Evaluators will mean that new ideas are few and far between, since they are likely to be quashed before being given a chance to air. This dampened spirit will affect the activities of others, meaning that creative individuals, like Plants, will be afraid to speak up for fear of having their ideas ridiculed or rejected out of hand. If such "paralysis by analysis" is left to continue, the organisation will soon find itself stagnating, and seemingly unable to account for its unmotivated workforce.

A sales company commonly hires Resource Investigators for their enthusiasm, persuasiveness and "gift of the gab." With such a lively staff and all phone lines buzzing, bosses might wonder why the profits are not as high as anticipated. In spite of the enthusiasm shown for landing the initial sale, goodwill is soon lost. Few structures will be in place for ensuring customer care and follow-up. Projects will seem to have been abandoned in mid-flow. Customers may feel that they have a great contact at the company, but will eventually become frustrated by their gradual loss of interest

A culture with too many Plants might also prove inefficient, but for very different reasons. It might be tempting to recruit Plants for their innovative, pioneering mentality and unconventional thinking. However, where too many Monitor Evaluators cause stagnation through over-criticism, Plant culture destabilises any structure already in place. A true Plant is a rare breed but worth holding out for – one brilliant idea far surpasses hundreds of indifferent or average ones.

Process industries are usually drawn to an Implementer culture, favouring employees who are efficient at getting the job done and loyal to the company. But the upshot of this may not be what is desired. Too many Implementers could mean an overstructured and inflexible culture. Routine procedures will leave little room for new ideas, and much will be sacrificed in the name of productivity. Employees will be given little scope for initiative. With Implementer managers interfering at operational levels, employees will be resentful that they are not respected or trusted to get on with the work.

In a Completer Finisher culture, high standards, rather than efficiency, take priority. Levels of anxiety are likely to be high, and, if there is little or no calming Co-ordinator influence, this anxiety could be severely detrimental to morale. At worst, the drive for perfectionism will turn into obsession. Employees are likely to work long hours, getting in early and staying late to make sure they have got every last detail right. Since so many people are competing to have the last say, a culture of penny-pinching or splitting hairs is likely to develop. Individuals will be eager to claim ownership of work and reluctant to delegate it. The price paid is that consultation will be rare, with individuals or departments operating as "lone rangers" without reference to each other.

Employing too many Specialists produces its own typical problems. The willingness to develop and maintain specialised knowledge might be highly desirable for a pharmaceutical company recruiting scientists and technicians, for example. But if there are no Shapers or Resource Investigators to drive the company forward, or consider what is needed in the market, individuals will become bogged down in project work, and over-protective of their areas of special interest.

Combination cultures

Knowing the culture of the organisation will give you insight into the likely advantages and pitfalls and how you can fit in and progress.

The tables below demonstrate the positive and negative features commonly produced by certain Team Role combinations:

Positive Features

Culture of Leaders	Culture Focus	Culture Type
Co-ordinators Team Workers	Development of Human Resources	Human Relations Model
Plants Resource Investigators	Expansion, Transformation	Open Systems Model
Completer Finishers Implementers	Consolidation, Equilibrium	Internal Process Model
Monitor Evaluators Shapers	Maximisation of Output, Competitiveness	Rational Goal Model

Negative Features

Culture of Leaders	Culture Focus	Culture Type
Co-ordinators Team Workers	Permissiveness Unproductive Discussion	Country Club
Plants Resource Investigators	Premature responsiveness	Tumultuous anarchy
Completer Finishers Implementers	Procedural sterility	Frozen bureaucracy
Monitor Evaluators Shapers	Exhaustive hostility	Oppressive Sweat Shop

The stronger the culture, the more resistant it will be to outsiders. However, sometimes it takes an outsider to provide a fresh perspective, which is why many companies use external PR agencies. Remember the adage: "In the kingdom of the blind, the one-eyed man is king." The one person who can see what is needed, if eventually recognised, will be much appreciated. In a "country club" scenario, practicality and organisation will stand out. In a "tumultuous anarchy," you need someone who thinks about fundamentals in an organised fashion. A "frozen bureaucracy" invites an enterprising individual to bring in new life and vitality. The "oppressive sweat shop" demands a person with a humanistic outlook, who can lead others to a more acceptable way of managing people. Of course, acting as a catalyst is far more demanding than fitting in with an existing culture. A successful change agent needs moral courage, a slice of luck and support from above.

Changing and influencing company culture

Changing a culture is a very demanding challenge. Adapting to an existing culture is a safer bet. There is however a third possibility. This third way is to foster and inspire changes in the company from within. That objective often proves more effective than trying to impose policies on an existing culture in the hope that they will stick. Experience tells us that, even if a noticeable change takes place, a culture comprising the same people will eventually return to its previous, organic state. The only perceptible consequence will be the growing disillusionment and frustration of those engaged in changing company culture.

If you find that you are able to change your company's culture for the better, all well and good. If you find that you are not in a position to start the campaign, but you feel that change would be beneficial, it is crucial to decide how important the relevant modifications are to you. If you feel you can live with the culture as it is, do your best to adapt to it, and accept the status quo. If you feel you won't be working at your best unless change comes about, it may be that the time has come for you to move on.

There are productive ways and means of managing culture, but it takes time and careful thought to change attitudes. The key is to start on a small scale, and not to expect too much too quickly. If you think you have found a more helpful process or behaviour, demonstrate your alternative methods. At first, you may only make a small impact in your immediate environment. However, if your idea works out, it will soon gain attention further afield in the organisation. However, do not be ostentatious. Have faith that the changes you make will receive the attention they deserve. Even if they are not adopted on a wider scale, at the very least your own way of working will have improved.

You can help yourself by making sure that any first initiative gains support from someone. You will feel the benefit of any alliance should you have to introduce a less than popular measure. Make sure that your own behaviour is always consistent and in line with any prospective change, so that you cannot be accused of hypocrisy. Be sure to remove any elements of personal gain which might result from the change, since these will lead others to treat your suggestions with suspicion and distrust. Be seen to be advocating changes for the benefit of the organisation alone, and you will reap the most important reward – of seeing that alteration introduced. It is important to note that the impetus for change does not have to be your own. If you see an influential person adopting a style of which you approve, be vocal in your support for them. By so doing, you will increase the chances of seeing this style adopted throughout the company.

To summarise:

- Each company culture is unique.

- Be aware of any Team Role culture and consider where you fit in.

- Think carefully before making changes – don't be afraid to start small.

The Belbin Guide to Succeeding at Work

CHAPTER SEVEN

Moving Forward In Your Career

Getting promoted

Once you have been offered a job in an organisation, no matter what your starting-point, you can make headway by volunteering yourself for opportunities as they arise. Display a "can do" attitude and announce yourself, because nobody else will do it for you. Although you should not expect instant results, your manager is likely to respect hard work and good performance. If you want to progress up the career ladder, you need to think about the types of behaviour that will single you out for promotion. With so much competition around, you will need to stand out from your colleagues. Five points need to be kept in mind.

Firstly, it is essential to be seen as proactive rather than simply reactive. This means coming up with suggestions, taking on work without being asked and taking a lead in conversations with others. However this needs to be done in a helpful way rather than by adopting a superior attitude.

Secondly, you will need to show that you are a good strategist rather than someone who functions only on an operational front. The higher you go in management, the more strategic thinking outweighs operational leadership.

Thirdly, use phrases that promote who you truly are. If you happen to be a Coordinator-Shaper, come out with phrases like "I thrive on responsibility." This will ensure you can be used to effect in accordance with your desires and abilities.

Fourthly, do a little bit more than you have been asked to do by your boss. This does not mean you have to put in masses of overtime which might not even be spotted or noticed by the boss, who, in all probability, was not there at the time. However, you can add value to the job you were given by doing a little more than is required. You will have to be careful, however, not to dip into the territories of others, which will not endear you to your work colleagues or your boss. Look instead for areas where opportunities exist or significant tasks have been forgotten.

Finally, and perhaps most importantly, tackle work that needs to be done rather than work that you fancy doing. People are appreciated who do the hard graft rather than cherry-pick what suits them best. Never be afraid to take on the most humble of jobs. It may not be mentioned at the time, but if you have a good boss, it will be rewarded at a later stage.

Promotion will ultimately depend on the level of competition, but you can help yourself by adjusting your own attitude. In essence you have got to look a better candidate than your colleagues – or external candidates – in the eyes of your manager. If you fail to win immediate selection, don't worry. Keep your ear to the ground and there will be other opportunities.

Bear in mind that the structure of the organisation may not be helping you to progress. Laurence J. Peter devised the 'Peter Principle' in 1968. He looked at three levels in an educational institution – the teacher, the Head of Department and the School Head. Being good at one level did not mean being good at a further level, for different skills apply at each. His specific observation in the educational field was found to hold a general truth. In a hierarchical organisation, individuals continue to be promoted by being competent until they eventually reach their "incompetence level." There they no longer warrant promotion, hence they remain where they are. This is why, in this theory, the world is full of incompetent people.

This theory stands up in structures where there is a rigid hierarchy, but when organisations move away from hierarchy and towards team working, everything changes. Individuals are no longer locked into set positions but will experience a variety of demands, which will allow them to display aptitude in different areas. They are therefore able to be promoted according to aptitude rather than becoming trapped on one layer of hierarchy, where incompetence at something will put their career on hold. Looking at work as a series of jobs, each with its own aptitude, therefore avoids the Peter Principle coming into effect.

Am I suited to management?

A manager is someone who seeks to deploy human, technical and financial resources to best effect in pursuit of an objective. In effect, it is a particular type of human skill for which individuals possess varying aptitudes. The confusion about the title of manager is that it also implies rank and salary in a hierarchical system. Pursuit of rank for its own sake is a dubious proposition. If a person does aspire to become a manager, it is important to come to terms with what managerial responsibilities entail and to have the confidence to know that one can fully measure up to its demands.

So what you must decide is whether or not this is a route for you and where you want to go. Will you be employed to best effect as a manager as defined above? Do you even want to take on the stress and responsibility that management entails? Or would you prefer continuing in your own field of expertise where you can do what you know you do well? If you enjoy doing what you do now, why change? Is it the money, the ambition or the status that is driving you forward to higher levels of management? Perhaps these reasons alone will not suffice. How do you even know if you will be good at management if you haven't tried it before?

Perhaps you ought to ask yourself another set of questions. Do you have a passion to become a manager? Do you think you will enjoy the challenge? Are you interested in allocating work to others? Do you enjoy dealing with other people's problems? If the answer is "no" to most of these, it is worth

The Belbin Guide to Succeeding at Work

asking yourself whether you really want to apply for a managerial post. After all, why get taken away from something you have an affinity for, in order to work at something you have none for? What is crucial is that you do what suits. If you are to become a manager, it is not you who ultimately chooses. It is someone else (also with a managerial role) who offers you a post. Presumably they only select you because they think you have aptitude and potential to become a manager. Your own view of your skills becomes irrelevant: it is others who will rate you. If you *are* still interested in becoming a manager, read on.

To summarise:

- When considering promotion, evaluate exactly what the job entails and whether you are suited.

- Remember that you might do better to strive for the position which will give you greatest personal fulfilment.

The Belbin Guide to Succeeding at Work

CHAPTER EIGHT

Entering into Management

A manager should be someone who recognises talents in the team and delegates work accordingly. Work to be distributed to others falls into one of two categories: tasks and responsibilities. A task is an item of work that necessarily has to be done. Passing responsibility to someone, however, indicates that the named person is held accountable for a particular outcome, irrespective of how it is discharged.

Allocating work

The distinction between these two types of work is important to observe because managers are the ones who carry responsibility. Some individuals thrive on responsibility; for others, it is a source of stress. Because responsibility leads us to blame ourselves if plans miscarry, those who perceive themselves as inadequate will suffer from anxiety. The wider the responsibility, the greater the possibility of mishap. Whatever mistakes are made, and whoever makes them, the person at the top will be held accountable.

What you will have to ask yourself is whether you are the sort of person who thrives on responsibility or whether it is something that will weigh heavily on your shoulders. Bear in mind that all the rank, status or remuneration in the world won't make you happy if you're always stressed in your job.

Good managers need to think of work not purely in terms of business, but in terms of the people in the team and how their abilities would best be used. This gives rise to a number of questions: should the manager undertake responsibility for everything? Or are some responsibilities better shared or passed on? Given that certain tasks have to be performed, should the method and procedure be precisely prescribed or should variation be allowed within certain guidelines?

The first thing to realise here is that delegating all work in the form of tasks will limit your scope, and that of your team. So it is important not only to delegate the task, but to recognise whether or not you can also delegate the responsibility.

Different management styles

It would be naïve to assume that there is one management style to which all must adhere. If you are to become a manager, you must look at the situation, the responsibilities in hand, and the people involved. With this information you can adopt a style that suits. In fact, successful managers are usually those who have fashioned their own unique style and have succeeded because they are playing a role which is natural to them and makes use of their talents.

Remember, your managerial position requires you to make certain decisions, rather than to simply follow a set of rules. Otherwise there would be no need for a manager. It is important, however, to ascertain where your responsibilities start and where they end. Working outside these boundaries could spell disaster.

It is a manager's job to facilitate progress or perhaps bring about change, but not to try and impose personal authority or an air of superiority over the team. A manager will gain respect over a period of time if they prove to be effective. Demanding respect for its own sake will only backfire. The art of managing lies in being self-aware and recognising where the skills of others in the team can be used to balance personal weaknesses.

Building yourself a talented team

First of all, you must consider talent in members of your team to be an asset and not a threat. As a manager, you will achieve recognition for having a talented team which functions well as a unit, rather than for being pre-eminent amongst them. It is a natural tendency to worry about other people's superior strengths because these can show you at a comparative disadvantage. Managers often surround themselves with acolytes. Leading a submissive team will give you an easy time, but will not yield the best results. People who are able and willing to give an opinion can be invaluable to managers.

Building and using your team correctly becomes increasingly significant as you progress to the upper echelons of management. You will need to delegate more responsibilities to others as complexities grow. Talented colleagues will wish to carry responsibilities in their own right, and this could cause conflict. Managers successful in their own team "territory" often find they cannot work effectively with others. This is where Team Role knowledge can help.

Humility versus ego

As a manager, perhaps one of greatest lessons to learn is the importance of humility. One's own ego may quite easily be tempted to enlarge itself with increased power and responsibility. Remember that self-praise is no praise.

As a manager, you are expected to make decisions. The higher you climb, the more important decisions become. However, growing self-confidence and self-importance does not add to the quality of decision-making. If you are going to shout, do so for the good of the company and not to advance your status. Should you make an incorrect decision, you would do better to admit it and backtrack. Excuses will not help. The more you make them, the more they will damage your credibility.

Finally, if you use the language of Team Roles, you can admit your weaknesses without inflicting any damage. Ironically, it is those weaknesses which can make you appreciated amongst your team. Furthermore, it gives everyone else a chance to be of use.

Although it may be a daunting proposition, it is important to realise that you will need to find a managerial approach that works for you. Refining this approach will involve an understanding of team dynamics and a lot of self-awareness. If sensitively handled, it will point you towards success. There is no "one size fits all" rule for aspiring managers, but there are a few pointers to take on board.

Ten tips for managers

1. Play to your strengths

Few successful managers are altogether free of faults, but you can achieve success by playing your strong suit well. Learning to manage yourself effectively is a prerequisite to managing others well. Here there are general lessons worth bearing in mind.

2. Ascertain how others see you

Self-flattery is a common device for self-promotion, but it is also the high road to the self-deception that precedes a fall. To foster good relationships with others, it is desirable to have regular feedback on how you are seen.

3. Don't confuse managing a business with managing people

Some talented business managers are exceptionally poor at managing people. Equally, some excellent people managers know little about managing process. Success in any of these fields often disguises weaknesses in other areas. If you are strong in one area, make sure you have a good ally in an adjacent field. The key to progress is not always to take the difficult road to self-improvement. A more reliable option is to take the shortcut by finding and working with people demonstrating the skills you lack.

4. Don't paint a sinking ship

Organisations with holes in their operating systems are bound to flounder. Concentrate on creating an improved structure of management and leave the finer details for later. A seaworthy ship rather than a smart ship is easier to steer in the right direction.

5. Prioritise good strategy over operational efficiency

It is preferable to do the right things inefficiently rather than the wrong things well. Complex operations only work effectively with the provision of adequate thinking time. So thinking should come before action.

6. It is better to appoint at leisure than to sack in haste or to live with a mistaken appointment

Taking meticulous care when making appointments is seldom a waste of time. A rushed decision taken in ten minutes can lead to several years of regret.

7. Endeavour to find the right peg for the right hole

Those who fail in one job may well succeed in another, if the correct appointment is made. Experience with the Belbin Job Requirement Exercise bears out the adage that there are "horses for courses."

8. Take an interest in all jobs

All jobs are deserving of managerial attention. People appreciate praise, and will accept criticism if it is focused on the task rather than the person.

9. Don't interfere too much

Managing is about delegation. Give someone autonomy over, as well as responsibility for, a job. Interfering and micro-management can diminish the desire to assume further responsibilities.

10. Make known your chosen style of management

Once you have established your strengths and weaknesses, announce to your team what you think you can contribute and what you expect from others.

The real test of managerial ability is whether a person can manage as well in one situation or industry as in another. The only way to find out is to initiate a move. Some managers of repute have done just that: they have succeeded because they have mastered the generalities of management. When managers take charge of their own careers they are in the business of learning, and can impart what they have learned to others.

To summarise:

- Delegate tasks and responsibilities to others.

- Surround yourself with a talented team.

- Be humble in a position of responsibility.

What now?

So what am I going to do differently on Monday morning? This is a question frequently asked by people having attended a management education course or company team-building event. If you have read *The Belbin Guide to Succeeding at Work*, even if not from cover to cover, we hope it will have given you a renewed ambition and desire to identify your current behaviours in your work environment – as well as other people's. Why is this important? Because success in a team begins with self-knowledge and understanding of others. Understanding things from your manager's point-of-view, for example, can set you apart even at interview. Team Roles can help gain mutual understanding, by providing a common language, and giving everyone a suitable part to play. If things do go wrong, Team Roles can provide a language of reconciliation. Armed with an objective frame of reference, you can avoid offence through misunderstanding and diffuse potentially volatile situations.

Wherever you go in your chosen career path, the way you behave will greatly influence your eventual position. There is the old adage "you are employed for what you know and fired for who you are". We all have our idiosyncrasies and human frailties. Indeed others like us not to be perfect. Ultimately, we just need to manage our weaknesses and project our strengths. The key is to approach work with enthusiasm and determination, but not to lose sight of yourself in the process. A healthy dose of realism is crucial to success.

GLOSSARY

The Job Feature Questionnaire

The JFQ is an open-ended questionnaire designed to measure the strength and direction of job motivation. It was designed to give an assessment of the relative strengths of individuals' most important job needs.

The responses are categorised below with a question against each category. Each question describes the underlying concept that the individual is considering. The range of questions covers virtually all possible responses.

J1	Appropriateness	Are my skills and aptitude right for the job?
J2	Task	Which particular bit of the job interests me?
J3	Structure	Do I know what I am doing in this job?
J4	Brain	Can I think in this job?
J5	People-	Will others frustrate me in this job?
J6	People+	Will I meet and deal with people?
J7	Variety	Is there scope to deal with different things?
L1	Values	Can I help people or improve society?
L2	Approval	Will I be liked if I do this job?
L3	Conditions	Am I happy with the hours and working conditions?
L4	Job Security	Will I have the job in the future?
L5	Enjoyment	Will I have fun in this job?
L6	Rejection of Pressure	Is there anything that sounds too difficult or onerous?

D1 Challenge   Will I be pushed to my limits?
D2 Activity   Will I be able to do things and be kept busy?
D3 Impact   Will I be able to have an effect on others?
D4 Initiative   Will there be scope for making my own decisions?
D5 Authority   Will I be able to order people about?
D6 Ambition   Will this job give opportunity to advance my career?

The three main categories are:

Job Content	Concern over the tasks or content of the job.
Lifestyle	Concern over what can be got out of the job in terms of the individual's enjoyment.
Drive	Concern that the job satisfies the need for managerial achievement.

Maslow and his Hierarchy of Needs

Abraham Maslow was an American psychologist born in Brooklyn in 1908. After gaining his PhD in psychology in 1934, he taught psychology to many leading 20th century psychologists. In 1951, becoming chairman of the psychology department at Brandeis University, he began his own theoretical research.

Maslow saw human beings' needs arranged like a ladder. The most basic needs, at the bottom, were physical – air, water, food, sex. Then came safety needs – security, stability – followed by psychological, or social needs – for belonging, love, acceptance. At the top of it all were the self-actualising needs – the need to fulfil oneself, to become all that one is capable of becoming. Maslow felt that unfulfilled needs lower on the ladder would inhibit the person from climbing to the next step. He pointed out that someone dying of thirst quickly forgets their thirst when they have no oxygen. People who were concerned with the higher needs were what he called self-actualising people. They had what he called "Peak experiences" – profound moments of love, understanding, happiness – when they felt more concerned with truth, justice, harmony, goodness.

Team Role Descriptions ~ In Summary

Team Role	Contribution	Allowable Weaknesses
Plant	Creative, imaginative, free-thinking. Generates ideas and solves difficult problems.	Ignores incidentals. Too preoccupied to communicate effectively.
Resource Investigator	Outgoing, enthusiastic, communicative. Explores opportunities and develops contacts.	Over-optimistic. Loses interest once initial enthusiasm has passed.
Co-ordinator	Mature, confident, identifies talent. Clarifies goals. Delegates effectively.	Can be seen as manipulative. Offloads own share of the work.
Shaper	Challenging, dynamic, thrives on pressure. Has the drive and courage to overcome obstacles.	Prone to provocation. Offends people's feelings.
Monitor Evaluator	Sober, strategic and discerning. Sees all options and judges accurately.	Lacks drive and ability to inspire others. Can be overly critical.
Teamworker	Co-operative, perceptive and diplomatic. Listens and averts friction.	Indecisive in crunch situations. Avoids confrontation.
Implementer	Practical, reliable, efficient. Turns ideas into actions and organises work that needs to be done.	Somewhat inflexible. Slow to respond to new possibilities.
Completer Finisher	Painstaking, conscientious, anxious. Searches out errors. Polishes and perfects.	Inclined to worry unduly. Reluctant to delegate.
Specialist	Single-minded, self-starting, dedicated. Provides knowledge and skills in rare supply.	Contributes only on a narrow front. Dwells on technicalities.

The Belbin Guide to Succeeding at Work

A selection of Belbin Reports

Belbin Team Role Reports	Brief Explanation:
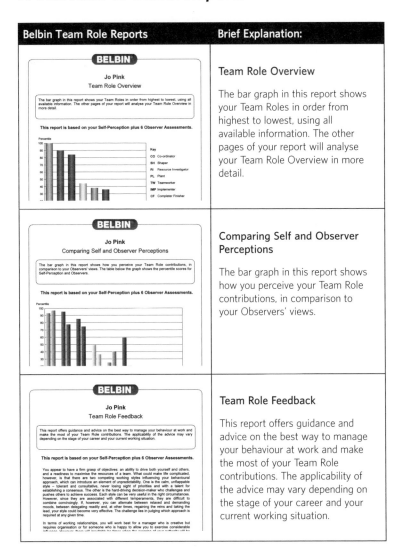	**Team Role Overview** The bar graph in this report shows your Team Roles in order from highest to lowest, using all available information. The other pages of your report will analyse your Team Role Overview in more detail.
	Comparing Self and Observer Perceptions The bar graph in this report shows how you perceive your Team Role contributions, in comparison to your Observers' views.
	Team Role Feedback This report offers guidance and advice on the best way to manage your behaviour at work and make the most of your Team Role contributions. The applicability of the advice may vary depending on the stage of your career and your current working situation.

Belbin reports can be used to:

- Enable individuals to form productive working relationships
- Select and develop high-performing teams
- Raise self-awareness and increase personal effectiveness
- Identify talent in the workplace

If you are interested in finding out how the Belbin reports can help you, your team or your organisation, please visit the Belbin website: www.belbin.com, or contact us at info@belbin.com

Further Resources from Belbin

Books by R. M. Belbin

Management Teams - Why They Succeed or Fail
ISBN: 978-0-7506-5910

Team Roles at Work
ISBN: 978-0-7506-2675

Beyond the Team
ISBN: 978-0-7506-4641

Website: **www.belbin.com**

DVD: **Fire, Toast and Teamwork**